W9-DAP-593

7.95
93
er
Burdett

Eastern
Europe

Editor
Julia Kirk
Design
Roland Blunk
Picture Research
Brigitte Arora
Production
Rosemary Bishop
Illustrations
Ron Hayward Associates

Consultant
John Mulanney
Head of European Studies,
Hugh Farringdon School,
Reading.

Page 6: the Alexanderplatz,
East Berlin.

Endpaper: Romanian women take a
break from their work in the
fields.

Cover picture of May Day
Parade in Prague by
Bo Bojesen.

Photographic Sources
Key to positions of illustrations:
(T) top, (C) centre, (B) bottom,
(L) left, (R) right, (M) middle.

ADN Zentralbild 42(BR), 47(TR)
Berolina Travel 10, 47(B), 50(R)
Nick Birch 21(TR), 46(B)
Black Theatre, Prague 33(L)
Bo Bojesen 11, 12(L), 13, 14, 15(TR),
  16, 17(T, ML, MR), 18, 19(BL,
  BR), 20(L), 21(TL), 22, 23, 25(TL,
  MR), 32(BR), 33(TL), 34(R),
  36(T), 37(B), 38, 39(TR), 40,
  41(BR, BL), 44, 45, 46(T), 47(TL),
  48(L, R), 49, 50(L), 51(BL, BR),
  endpaper
Camera Press (30R), 31(B), 33(BR),
  39(TL)
J. Allan Cash 42(BL)
Czechoslovak Travel Bureau, London
  9(T)
Imperial War Museum 30(L)
Keystone Press 29(BR), 31(TL, TR),
  42(TL)
Kobal Collection 33(TL)
The Mansell Collection 28(L)
Military Museum, Belgrade 27(BL)
New Albania Society 32(BL)
Chris Niedenthal contents page, 12(R),
  15(TL), 17(B), 19(T), 20(R),
  35(TL, TR, B), 36(M, B),
  37(TL, TR), 39(B), 41(T), 43

Polish Tourist Information Centre
  (Orbis) 51(T)
Suddeutscher Verlag 26, 27(TR, BR),
  28(R), 29(T, BL)
The Tate Gallery 33(TR)
Yugoslav National Tourist Office 9(M)
ZEFA 9(B), 15(B), 21(B), 25(TR),
  35(BL)

First published 1979
Macdonald Educational Ltd.,
Holywell House,
Worship Street,
London EC2A 2EN

© Macdonald Educational
Limited, 1979

Published in the United
States by Silver Burdett
Company, Morristown, N.J.
1979 Printing

Library of Congress
Catalog Card No. 79-65841
ISBN 0-382-06326-0

Eastern Europe

by

Peter Barker

Macdonald Educational

Contents

Eight different lands

Mountains and plains

Eight countries make up the socialist bloc of states we call 'Eastern Europe'. In order of size these are Poland, Yugoslavia, Romania, Czechoslovakia, Bulgaria, the German Democratic Republic (GDR), Hungary and Albania. Poland is a bit larger than Great Britain, while Albania is about the size of Belgium.

Altogether, these countries cover about one third of the area of Europe as a whole (excluding the Soviet Union), and extend from the Baltic Sea in the north to the Black Sea in the east and the Adriatic Sea in the south.

Eastern Europe is an area of many contrasts. The northern parts of the GDR and Poland form part of the Northern European Plain, which stretches from Holland to the Soviet Union. Here the land is flat and mainly used for agriculture. Czechoslovakia is a mixture of fertile plains and high mountain ranges, such as the High Tatras. Although there are some low hills in the north of Hungary, near Lake Balaton, the major part of the country is dominated by the *Puszta* or Great Hungarian Plain, where herds of horses roam the wide open spaces.

Romania is a mountainous land, except for the eastern coastal strip and the Danube Plain in the south. A large part of Bulgaria is also mountainous, but there are two fertile plains, separated by the Balkan Mountains, and a beautiful stretch of coastline on the Black Sea. This area is a favourite holiday resort in the summer for people from all over Eastern Europe.

Extremes of climate

The climate of Eastern Europe varies considerably. In the northern and central areas the weather is cold in winter and warm in summer, while the coastal areas of Yugoslavia and Albania enjoy a Mediterranean climate, with mild, rainy winters and dry, hot summers. Some areas, especially in the central and eastern regions, are very cold in winter, with a fairly low rainfall over the whole of the year.

8

▲ The High Tatra mountains in Czechoslovakia offer some of the most dramatic scenery in Eastern Europe. Together with the Low Tatra mountains to the south, they form the western end of the Carpathian Mountains, which stretch south-east through the U.S.S.R. to Romania.

◄ Dubrovnik is one of the most popular tourist resorts on the Adriatic coast of Yugoslavia. Mountains come down to the sea and form many deep-water inlets which make excellent ports, of which Dubrovnik is one.

▼ The Hungarian Plain (Puszta) covers most of the eastern part of Hungary.

The crossroads of Europe

Early settlers

Since early times central and eastern Europe have been at the crossroads of the trade routes between western Europe, Asia and the Middle East. They have also been at the centre of the movement of people across the European land mass.

The forefathers of the present inhabitants of Eastern Europe settled there mainly between the fifth and tenth centuries A.D., after they had been driven out of their homelands.

The Slavs, who form the largest racial group today, originally came from the Pripet marshes in central Russia, but they were forced westward by the attacks of the Huns from the east. By the year 1000 A.D., the Slavs had split up into different groups, including Poles, Czechs and Slovaks, Serbs and Croats and Bulgarians.

The Hungarians, a nomadic race of horsemen, originally came from the steppes of central Asia and settled on the central plain of Eastern Europe from the ninth century onwards.

In the south, the major influence in early times was the Byzantine Empire, which grew from the eastern half of the Roman Empire after it split in two in 395 A.D. This empire continued to exist until its capital, Constantinople (later called Istanbul), was captured by the Turks in 1455.

The Turks then steadily extended their influence north through the Balkans into Hungary and Romania, creating the Ottoman Empire. The Turks were, however, soon pushed back into the Balkans and German and Hungarian influences again became dominant with the creation of the Austro-Hungarian Empire.

The Jewish influence has also been strong in Eastern Europe. Jews began moving into the central areas of Poland and Lithuania from the twelfth century onwards after religious persecution drove them out of Germany, France, England and Spain. They formed a large part of the populations of Poland, Romania, Hungary and Czechoslovakia until their attempted extermination by Hitler during the Second World War.

The races of Eastern Europe today

The racial groups of Eastern Europe are more settled today than ever.

The Slavs are split into two main groups: the western Slavs, comprising the Poles, Sorbs, Czechs and Slovaks; and the southern Slavs, comprising the Slovenes, Croats, Serbs, Macedonians and Bulgarians.

The Hungarians now occupy a much smaller area than they did at the height of the Austro-Hungarian Empire. In fact, over two and a half million Hungarians are citizens of other states, and over half of these live in Romania. There is also a large minority of Germans in Romania, the descendants of German settlers who came to the Transylvanian Alps in the thirteenth century.

▲ The racial features of many Poles and East Germans are similar to those of the Scandinavians, with blond hair and fair skins. Here we see a group of children in the GDR.

▶ The central position of Eastern Europe has made it open to population movements from all directions. The most important migrations have been the Slavs and Magyars from the east, the Germans from the west and north, and the Turks from the south-east.

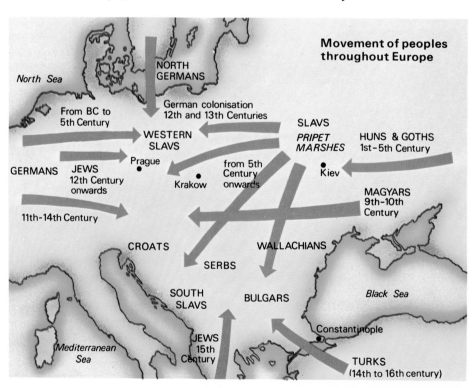

Movement of peoples throughout Europe

North Sea

NORTH GERMANS

From BC to 5th Century

German colonisation 12th and 13th Centuries

SLAVS
PRIPET MARSHES

HUNS & GOTHS 1st-5th Century

WESTERN SLAVS

Prague

GERMANS JEWS 12th Century onwards

Krakow

from 5th Century onwards

Kiev

MAGYARS 9th-10th Century

11th-14th Century

CROATS

WALLACHIANS

SERBS

SOUTH SLAVS

BULGARS

Black Sea

Mediterranean Sea

JEWS 15th Century

Constantinople

TURKS (14th to 16th century)

▶ Romanian peasants in traditional dress. Romanians are descended from the Roman settlers of 2,000 years ago. Their language has therefore developed from Latin, like Italian.

◀ There are still a large number of gypsies in Eastern Europe, especially in Romania and Bulgaria. These are gypsy girls in Romania.

▼ An Albanian, now resident in Yugoslavia, watches his horse being shod. Over a million Albanians live in Yugoslavia. This man wears the traditional Albanian cap, or *cula*, made of white wool.

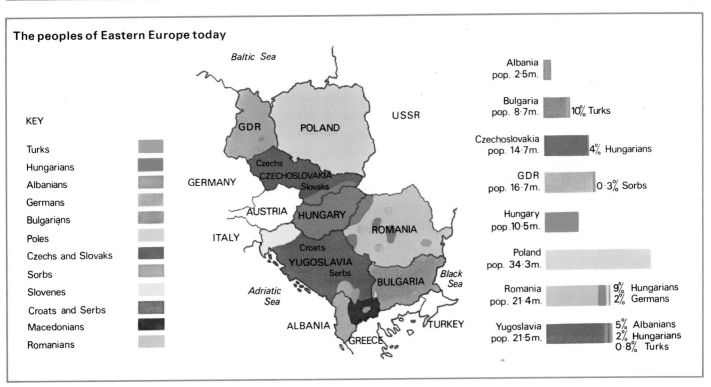

The peoples of Eastern Europe today

KEY

Turks
Hungarians
Albanians
Germans
Bulgarians
Poles
Czechs and Slovaks
Sorbs
Slovenes
Croats and Serbs
Macedonians
Romanians

Baltic Sea

GDR | POLAND | USSR

GERMANY

Czechs
CZECHOSLOVAKIA
Slovaks

AUSTRIA

ITALY

HUNGARY

ROMANIA

Croats

YUGOSLAVIA
Serbs

BULGARIA

Adriatic Sea

Black Sea

ALBANIA

GREECE

TURKEY

Albania
pop. 2·5m.

Bulgaria
pop. 8·7m.   10% Turks

Czechoslovakia
pop. 14·7m.   4% Hungarians

GDR
pop. 16·7m.   0·3% Sorbs

Hungary
pop.10·5m.

Poland
pop. 34·3m.

Romania
pop. 21·4m.   9% Hungarians
                     2% Germans

Yugoslavia
pop. 21·5m.   5% Albanians
                     2% Hungarians
                     0·8% Turks

Changing patterns of family life

The move to the towns

With rapid industrialization, many country dwellers have moved to the towns. This has caused extreme housing shortages in the towns and left some villages almost deserted. There is, in fact, one village in Hungary – Gyurufu – which has become totally empty!

Families have also begun to split up into smaller units. In the past it was usual for three generations of a family to live together – grandparents, parents and children. It is now more common for children to move away from home in their late teens or early twenties.

Most of the big towns in Eastern Europe have seen a large increase in population over the last thirty years. This, combined with the destruction of many buildings during the Second World War, has meant that all the major towns of Eastern Europe have suffered from an acute housing shortage. Some towns, such as Budapest and East Berlin, have attempted to improve the situation by restricting the number of people who are allowed to move to these towns.

The overwhelming majority of people living in towns rent flats. It is very unusual to find individual families occupying whole houses, since pre-war houses are now mostly split up into flats and almost all new housing is in the form of flats. By western standards the flats are rather small, with a family of four living in a two- or three-room flat with kitchen and bathroom. But compared with western Europe, the rents are extremely low.

Family spending

An Eastern European would on average spend about five per cent of his income on rent and about fifteen per cent on his total housing costs, including fuel and furniture. In western Europe, the average worker would expect to pay at least twenty per cent of his income on rent and on heating costs. On the other hand, the Eastern European spends a higher percentage of his income on food since, although basic foodstuffs such as bread are very cheap, other foodstuffs, such as meat and coffee, are extremely expensive.

It is very common in Eastern Europe for both parents to go out to work, and this means that life is very hectic, particularly since work tends to start early in the morning.

The fact that most wives work should mean that husbands take their share of the housework, but a survey carried out in the GDR in 1968 showed that women still spent an average of forty-eight hours a week on housework, while the men spent only seven hours. It will probably take some time, however, for the traditional role of women in the home to change in order to adapt to the changing patterns of society.

▲ It is still common for three generations of a family to live together. This has, however, become more difficult in towns, where families often have to live in small flats. This picture shows a family in Hungary where half the population still live in the country, and where many houses are privately owned.

► Although there is still a general housing shortage in Eastern Europe, many new estates have been built in the last ten years, like this one in Warsaw. All estates have play areas for children.

Family spending	Food	Housing, Fuel	Clothing	Culture & Recreation	Other
Poland	38.7%	12.2%	14.4%	6.7%	28%
Hungary	34.5%	14.4%	13%	6.6%	31.5%
France	25.9%	22.2%	8.7%	8.6%	34.6%
Yugoslavia	35%	15%	9%	12%	29%
W. Germany	20.3%	28.3%	8.9%	7.3%	35.2%

◀ Eastern Europeans spend a larger proportion of their budgets on food. This is because certain foodstuffs, such as meat and coffee, are far more expensive than in western Europe, although basic foods, such as bread and potatoes, are cheaper. Clothing is also more expensive.

▼ Although more and more families have washing machines in Romania, some women still wash the clothes in the traditional way — in the river. The river also provides an ideal opportunity for the weekly car wash!

▲ A Polish family in their kitchen. Flats are usually quite small. Kitchens and living-rooms often have to be used as bedrooms as well.

▶ Many Poles still live in the countryside. Most of the farms are still privately owned, with families living in the traditional one-storey farmhouses. The facilities are usually not as good as in the towns, but the family has much more space.

Shops and shopping

▲ The currencies of Eastern Europe cannot be directly converted into a western currency, apart from the Yugoslav dinar. Except for the East German mark and Yugoslav dinar, each currency has an official bank rate of exchange, and a tourist rate which is much higher. The table below gives an idea of the values of the currencies against the British pound.

Albania	20.5	new lek
Bulgaria	2.4	leva
Czechoslovakia	17.06	kcs (crowns)
GDR	4.0	ostmark
Hungary	36.0	florint
Poland	58.0	zloty
Romania	25.0	lei
Yugoslavia	33.5	dinar

How prices compare

	UK	GDR	W Germany
(car)	£2,500	£5,000	£3,000
(television)	£80	£400	£112
(washing-machine)	£60	£150	£80

▲ The prices of consumer goods are much higher in Eastern Europe. Wage rates are lower in the GDR than, for example, in West Germany or Britain, so that a worker must work even more hours to buy a car than a similar worker in western Europe. There is also still a waiting list for cars.

▶ Clothes bought at shops tend to be much more expensive in the communist countries of Eastern Europe, so many people make their own. or buy them from private stalls, like this one in Bulgaria.

Private enterprise and the State

The majority of shops in Eastern Europe are owned and run by the State. When compared with shops in western Europe, these can look rather drab, with a much smaller range of goods on display. But where there have been large redevelopments of town centres, such as the Alexanderplatz in Berlin, large new supermarkets have been built and offer the shopper a wide range of goods. The availability of consumer goods, such as televisions and washing-machines, has also improved over the last few years, since governments have allowed more of these goods to be produced.

However, there are still a number of shops which are owned privately. These tend to be the smaller shops and are very often those which offer a specific service, such as shoe-mending or barber's shops.

There is also a large number of open-air markets, where peasants sell the produce grown on their own plots of land. In Poland and Yugoslavia, private farmers have to deliver a certain amount of their produce to state-run shops through the official organizations, but they are also allowed to sell a certain amount privately.

Certain foods, such as eggs, are easier to get in the private markets, but prices are higher than in the price-controlled state shops. Prices in general are, however, more stable than in western Europe, since many goods are subsidized by the State. This means that the consumer in Eastern Europe does not pay the real price for a particular article. Rates of inflation have therefore tended to be much lower than in other parts of the world.

Standard of living

In general the standard of living in Eastern Europe is not as high as in western Europe, although it has recently been calculated that the standard of living in the GDR is higher than in Britain and Italy. But the GDR is some way ahead of the other countries in Eastern Europe and still cannot compete with West Germany or some of the Scandinavian countries.

Food shortages also present a problem in Eastern Europe. Many vegetables and fruits are only in the shops at certain times of the year, since the governments are reluctant to spend a lot of foreign currency on importing seasonal foodstuffs from abroad.

Meats also may often be in short supply. Poland, for example, is one of the world's largest producers of meat, yet it is sometimes difficult to buy various kinds of meat there because a large proportion of the meat produced is exported to bring in foreign currency. Often shoppers face long queues to buy particular items they really want.

◄ A modern department store in Brasov, Romania. Most large towns in Eastern Europe now have large supermarkets and department stores in their shopping centres.

► Sausages, especially garlic sausages, are one of the favourite foods of Eastern Europe. This shop in Prague, Czechoslovakia, seems to be especially popular.

▼ A private, open-air market in Hungary. Each peasant family is allowed to keep a small plot for growing fruit and vegetables, which can then be sold privately.

Working in Eastern Europe

Working in industry

The factory in Eastern Europe provides many facilities and services which would not be supplied in western Europe. For example, there are crèches and kindergartens where a working mother can leave her children. This is particularly important in a country like the GDR where over eighty per cent of women of working age have jobs.

The worker very often goes on holiday with his family to a hotel which is run by his trade union, and the factory also organizes sports facilities and leisure centres which can be used by the whole family. It also helps its workers to find a flat and provides a whole range of other services which in Britain would be organized by local authorities.

The trade unions have a very different role in Eastern Europe from the West. They are in charge of all social security funds, such as sick pay. They also ensure that safety regulations in the factory are observed by both the management and the work force. At the same time they cooperate with the management on planning and make sure that production targets are kept. They can also help workers who feel that they have been unjustly treated by the management.

Conditions of work

The wages of industrial workers are quite high compared with other workers although they seem rather low by western standards. The highest wages are paid in the GDR, which is by far the most successful country economically in Eastern Europe. Bulgaria, Yugoslavia and Albania have the lowest wages. It is difficult to compare these wages directly with those of western Europe, since many things, such as housing, are cheaper in Eastern Europe.

Most of the countries used to have a six-day working week, but it is normal now to have a five-day working week of about forty hours. Workers are now also paid bonuses based on the profits of their factory. These incentive schemes were mostly introduced in the late 1960s, except in Yugoslavia, where they were introduced earlier.

The right to work

Eastern Europe does not suffer from one of the major problems of western Europe's economy – unemployment. All the constitutions of the individual countries state that every citizen has a right and duty to work.

There are also very few strikes in Eastern Europe. It is argued that since the economy is mainly owned by the State in the name of the workers, they would be strking against themselves. There have, however, been some outbreaks of strikes, for example in the GDR in 1953 and in Poland in 1956 and 1970-71, when grievances were not recognized.

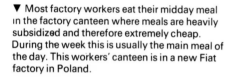

▼ Most factory workers eat their midday meal in the factory canteen where meals are heavily subsidized and therefore extremely cheap. During the week this is usually the main meal of the day. This workers' canteen is in a new Fiat factory in Poland.

▲ Polish workers learning a foreign language in a language laboratory. Education at work is a very important aspect of Eastern European life.

◄ Because industrial expansion has been so rapid, much industrial plant is very modern, like this new chemical processing plant in Yugoslavia.

► A Hungarian factory worker. It is much more common for women in Eastern Europe to have jobs normally done by men in western Europe.

Children in crèches and kindergartens

47.2%	Bulgaria
70.9%	G.D.R.
47.5%	Hungary
36.1%	Czechoslovakia
37.2%	Romania
24.9%	Poland

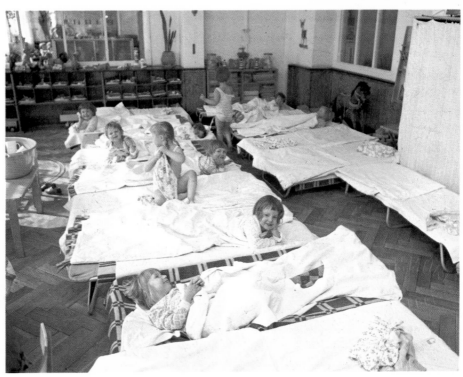

▲ The GDR has the best provision of crèches and kindergartens in Eastern Europe, but the other countries are still ahead of most other countries in Europe. Many crèches are situated at people's places of work.

► Children are brought by their mothers or fathers to work and left in the factory nursery for the day. The children can then be collected by the parents after work.

Youth movements

Young people's organizations

Youth movements play a very important role in the way of life of Eastern Europe. There are two main groups, almost totally modelled on the Soviet system.

The Pioneers is a group for young children from primary school age up to early teens. The movement is organized by the Communist Party and aims to educate the children in socialist values. Each summer thousands of children spend several weeks at a Pioneer camp where all kinds of sporting and leisure activities are organized for them.

During the rest of the year Pioneers are involved in such activities as helping old people and keeping their own villages tidy.

The Pioneer movement also prepares children for the Young Communist Movement which they can usually enter at the age of fourteen. This organization is the youth section of the Communist Party, and plays an important part in the political life of each country. In Hungary it is called the Communist Youth Union, in Yugoslavia the Federation of Yugoslav Youth and in Poland the Polish Socialist Youth Union.

Other youth organizations not connected with the Communist Party include the Scouts, which are popular in several of the countries of Eastern Europe. Poland has nearly three million members and the Scouts are also popular in Czechoslovakia.

Western influences

In the late 1950s and early 1960s western beat music was very much disapproved of by the governments of Eastern Europe. Records of such groups as the Beatles and Rolling Stones were banned from radio and there was also strong official disapproval of beat clubs and discotheques.

Nowadays the situation is different. Pop records are available in most Eastern European countries and there are now emerging many home-grown beat groups. Sometimes West German pop stars give concerts in the GDR and appear on GDR television.

Many opportunities for leisure

Apart from the facilities offered by the official youth organizations there is a wide range of leisure activities open to young people, especially sports. Clubs thrive in the various countries with sports ranging from chess to wrestling.

Cultural activities are also strongly encouraged and there are many youth orchestras and choirs, as well as youth theatres and artists' circles.

Hard work, whether at school, university or at work, is greatly encouraged and together with the many opportunities for leisure activities, keeps young people in Eastern Europe fully occupied.

▲ Young Eastern Europeans are often called upon to commemorate the liberation of their countries by the Soviet Union in 1945. These Czechoslovak Pioneers are laying a wreath to commemorate the liberation of Prague.

▶ The Youth organizations in communist countries of Eastern Europe often have to provide volunteers to help with different kinds of manual work. Here members of the Federation of Yugoslav Youth are helping to dig ditches.

▲ University students are not allowed to lose contact with normal working life. This group of students is helping with the harvest in central Poland during the summer vacation.

▲ In Hungary pioneers run a whole railway system for tourists. The only job done by adults is driving the steam-engines!

◀ A record shop in Yugoslavia. Western pop music is very popular amongst young people in Eastern Europe. In the fifties and sixties it was difficult to buy records by western groups. Now there are many on sale.

New methods of farming

Reorganizing the land

Agricultural conditions vary widely in Eastern Europe and differences in physical geography and climate have strongly influenced the development of agriculture. In the north where the land is flat it is much easier to create large farms, while in the mountainous regions of the south and east, large-scale farming has proved very difficult. So many variations in conditions meant that, after the great upheavals of 1939-45, farming had to be completely reorganized.

Collective farms based on the Soviet idea were introduced. The most common collective farm is the *kolkhoz*, in which the peasant's land, machinery and most of his animals become the collective property of the farm. He is allowed to keep a limited number of animals and a small garden plot to grow vegetables.

The state farm (*sovkhoz*) is more common in the Soviet Union than in Eastern Europe, but in Czechoslovakia and Romania they do account for one third of all land. These farms are owned and financed by the State, and the peasants are paid a fixed wage as in a factory. On a *kolkhoz* the farmer is paid according to how many days he has worked and how much money the farm has earned collectively.

Private farming is still important in most countries, especially Poland and Yugoslavia where the bulk of production comes from private farms.

Even in Romania, where a large amount of the land has been collectivized, nearly forty per cent of all produce comes from private land.

Although private farming is tolerated and sometimes encouraged, farmers very often have to wait until collective farms have been supplied before they receive their supplies. Much of their produce must be sold direct to the State, but they are allowed to sell part of their produce privately at open markets.

Produce of Eastern Europe

Eastern Europe produces a wide range of agricultural products. Particularly important are wheat and barley, sugar beet and potatoes. Maize is also a very important crop in Yugoslavia, Romania and Hungary. Poland is famous for its meat products, a large proportion of which is exported.

Productivity in Eastern Europe is still below western standards. Investment in agriculture has been low compared to industry, and this has meant that farms are still under-mechanized. As a result wheat and milk yields are lower than the average for Europe as a whole, except in the GDR, Czechoslovakia and Bulgaria.

There has been a rapid growth in production in the GDR and Bulgaria overall, but otherwise collective farming has not yet brought about the great upsurge in production which was hoped for.

▲ Although most farms in Poland are privately owned, there are a number of state farms where the level of mechanization is much higher than in the private sector. State farms are also usually much larger.

▶ Methods on private farms have not changed as much as on state and collective farms. This private farm is south of Warsaw in Poland.

▲ Albanian peasant women hoe the land using tools which have not changed for centuries. Albania is now making a determined effort to modernize its farming methods.

◀ Flocks of sheep in Yugoslavia are often tended by the younger members of the family. These sheep have been marked with the national symbol of Yugoslavia.

▼ Agricultural workers on a collective farm in Hungary. Most Hungarian farms are collective farms. Only about thirteen per cent of the total cultivated area is farmed privately.

Railways and waterways

Roads and railways

Railways are still the most important form of mass transport in Eastern Europe. The majority of freight traffic between the countries is still carried by rail and this has been made easier by the introduction of containers, especially in the GDR. There has also been modernization, such as the electrification of large sections of track in all of the countries, and the GDR and Czechoslovakia have started to use computers to operate switchboards and railway junctions.

Roads in Eastern Europe are not particularly good. There are very few motorways and the surfaces of the other main roads are often bumpy. The major motorways are, in fact, in Yugoslavia and in the GDR, where the autobahns were built in the late 1930s! This means that the main roads are often crowded with lorries and are rather slow.

Tourist traffic has also increased on the major holiday routes. This growth in private car traffic has been particularly noticeable in the 1970s. In the past, governments were reluctant to put too much investment into producing private cars when buses and lorries were far more valuable to the economy. This attitude has changed somewhat recently, and car production in Eastern Europe has risen a great deal in the last five years. However, there are fewer privately owned cars than in the West.

Water and air transport

Canals and rivers have traditionally provided important transport routes. There are two main waterway systems in Eastern Europe. In the north the Mittelland canal links the Rhine with the Elbe, the Spree and the Oder, so barge traffic can travel from Holland and West Germany into the GDR and Poland.

Poland itself has a kind of circular waterway system in which two main rivers, the Oder and the Vistula, are linked. This means that goods from the Baltic ports of Szczecin and Gdansk can be shipped right to the south of Poland. There is also a proposal to link the Oder and the Danube so that barges could travel from the Black Sea ports in the south to the Baltic ports in the north.

The Danube is by far the most important waterway of Eastern Europe, since it is navigable from Ulm in West Germany to the Black Sea. Now that the new canal in West Germany is completed, linking the Danube with the Main and the Rhine, it is possible to ship goods from the North Sea to the Black Sea.

Air transport has also expanded rapidly, especially passenger traffic. Each country has its own airline, operating international as well as internal flights, although the majority of international flights are within Eastern Europe itself, including the Soviet Union.

▲ A horse-drawn cart in Bulgaria. The old methods of transport are still common in the southern part of Eastern Europe.

► Traffic jams are a recent sight in the cities. The increase in car ownership over the last five years has brought this problem to many of the towns, such as Budapest, above.

▲ Wenceslas Square in Prague. Trams are a frequent sight in the towns and are considered to to be a cheap and efficient form of public transport.

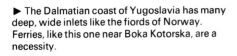

▲ Private cars are still very expensive to buy but motorbikes and bicycles are a common form of individual transport.

► The Dalmatian coast of Yugoslavia has many deep, wide inlets like the fiords of Norway. Ferries, like this one near Boka Kotorska, are a necessity.

The Danube – artery of Eastern Europe

The Danube as a frontier

Historically, the Danube has been very important as a barrier against invading armies. For many centuries, it formed the eastern boundary of the Roman empire. Budapest stands on the site of the Roman fortress of Aquincum, built to repel Barbarian invaders. Today the Danube is a busy and thriving waterway, acting as a link between the countries it passes through.

A river at work

The Danube is the second longest river in Europe, 2,864 kilometres in length. Only the Volga river in the Soviet Union is longer. In 1971 it was estimated that over 4,000 vessels were operating on the Danube, handling forty-seven million tons of cargo.

Many of the towns along the banks of the Danube are, of course, mainly important as ports, particularly for cereals and timber. Important in this respect are Komarno in Czechoslovakia, Komaron in Hungary, Vukovar in Yugoslavia, Vidin in Bulgaria, and Zimnicea in Romania.

There are also a number of ship-building towns, especially the Romanian ports of Orsova, Turnu Severin and Oltenita which specialize in barges and pleasure cruisers.

Apart from this there are a number of important industrial towns, the most interesting of which is the Hungarian town of Dunaujvaros, which has the largest iron and steel works in Hungary (The Danube Iron Works). This huge industrial complex and the adjoining town were not built until 1950 as part of the first Hungarian Five-Year Plan. Another important industrial town is Turnu Magurele, where there is a large chemical works.

Other significant economic centres are Bratislava, the capital of Slovakia; Budapest, the capital of Hungary, and Belgrade, the capital of Yugoslavia.

▲ The Danube traditionally forms a rough dividing line between the southern Slavs (Croatians, Serbs and Bulgarians) and the Romanians and Hungarians, who are both non-Slav races. Today it acts as a national frontier for a large part of its course through Eastern Europe.

In the past there were many disputes between the countries bordering the Danube, but today these countries are working together to improve the Danube as a shipping route. It is hoped that the building of new canals will help to increase the volume of cargo traffic, which is still low compared to that of the Rhine.

▲ Barges pass through the lock at the Iron Gates barrage, near Turnu Severin. These are the last straits on the Danube before the Black Sea and have always caused navigational problems. Here the Danube becomes much narrower as it flows between the Transylvanian Alps and the Balkan Mountains.

Ships used to be moved upstream against the strong current with the help of a steam engine which ran along the Yugoslav bank. Now the problems have been removed by a hydro-electric scheme which controls the flow of water. The scheme is a joint Yugoslav-Romanian project and is one of the largest in Eastern Europe.

▲ Budapest is one of the most beautiful cities on the Danube. Originally it was two towns, Buda on the right bank of the river and Pest on the left bank. It became a single town in 1872.

► The Danube divides into many rivers and streams before it flows into the Black Sea. The delta provides an excellent habitat for many rare birds and plants. The famous Beluga caviar comes from the sturgeon of the delta.

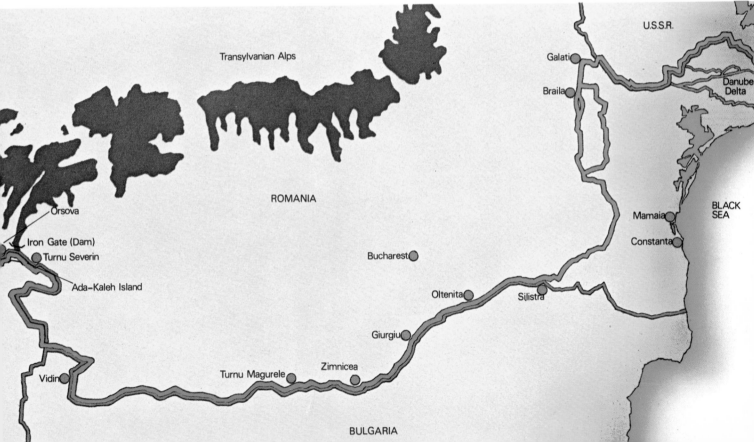

Transylvanian Alps

U.S.S.R.

Galati

Braila

Danube Delta

Orsova

Iron Gate (Dam)

Turnu Severin

Ada-Kaleh Island

ROMANIA

BLACK SEA

Mamaia

Constanta

Bucharest

Oltenita

Silistra

Giurgiu

Vidin

Turnu Magurele

Zimnicea

BULGARIA

Two Empires

Eastern Europe in 1815

Austro-Hungarian Empire

Ottoman Empire

PRUSSIA
Berlin
Warsaw
GERMAN STATES
SILESIA
BOHEMIA
Prague
SWITZERLAND
MORAVIA
Vienna
Pest
SLOVAKIA
RUSSIA
Belgrade
SERBIA
Bucharest
WALLACHIA
Black Sea
Constantinople
THE BALKANS

▲ After the defeat of Napoleon in June 1815, all the Great Powers of Europe met in Vienna to establish the frontiers of central Europe. The Congress of Vienna confirmed the position of Austria as the dominant force in central and Eastern Europe.

▼ In 1878 the Great Powers met in Berlin to decide the frontiers in south-eastern Europe after the defeat of the Turks by the Russians.

The Ottoman Empire in 1878

Budapest
AUSTRIA–HUNGARY
BOSNIA
HERZEGOVINA
Belgrade
SERBIA
ROMANIA
Bucharest
BULGARIA
Sofia
RUMELIA
OTTOMAN EMPIRE
MACEDONIA
ALBANIA
Constantinople
GREECE

Part of the Austro-Hungarian Empire after 1908

Became part of Bulgaria in 1885

The divisions of Eastern Europe

During the eighteenth and nineteenth centuries eastern and central Europe were divided into three major areas. The north was dominated by the German states (especially Prussia), Poland and the Russian Empire and in the south the Ottoman (Turkish) Empire covered most of the Balkans.

In the north Prussia expanded eastwards along the Baltic Sea, taking over the whole of the coastline as far as the Russian border. A unified German state under the leadership of Prussia was created in 1871.

After the withdrawal of the Turks from Hungary in 1699, Austria and Hungary were united under the Hapsburg Empire. For the next two centuries this empire dominated the central area of Eastern Europe.

From the fifteenth century, the Turks had been the major power in the south, with control over important ports on the Adriatic and Black Seas as well as over the mineral resources of Wallachia. But in the nineteenth century the Turkish Empire began to crumble. By 1914, Turkey had lost control of all its territory on the European continent, except for a small area around Constantinople.

The causes of war

The bitter rivalry between the Great Powers in the Balkans, especially between Austria and Russia, was one of the major causes of the outbreak of the First World War. In June 1914, the heir to the Austrian throne, Franz Ferdinand, was murdered in his open carriage by a Bosnian student in the streets of Sarajevo in Bosnia.

Although the Serbian government was not directly involved in the assassination, Austria accused Serbia of stirring up political unrest in its territories and in July 1914 declared war on Serbia. This marked the beginning of the First World War.

◀ The Janissaries formed the first Turkish regular army. Originally they were Christian prisoners forced to adopt the Turks' religion. In peacetime they acted as a police force and the sultan's bodyguard, in war they were foot soldiers. They were disbanded in 1826, because they were involved in conspiracies against the sultan.

▶ Abdul Hamid II (1842-1918) ruled the Ottoman Empire as sultan from 1876-1909. In 1876 he set aside the constitution which had just been proclaimed and ruled as a despot. He was deposed by the young Turks in 1909.

▲ A stamp commemorating the assassination of Archauke Franz Ferdinand and his wife.

▶ On 27th June 1914 the heir to the Austrian throne, Archduke Franz Ferdinand, and his wife were murdered while on a visit to Sarajevo in Bosnia, at that time part of the Austrian Empire. Austria accused Serbia of being involved in stirring up unrest against Austrian rule and declared war on Serbia.

▼ The assassin was a Bosnian student, Gavrilo Princip. He was a member of a secret organization called *The Black Hand,* which was opposed to Austrian rule.

The breakdown of democracy

The collapse of the old order

The defeat of the German Empire and the Austro-Hungarian Empire in 1918 marked the end of the old political order in central Europe.

Poland was made into an enlarged, independent state and gained a strip of land known as the Danzig corridor. Danzig (Gdansk) was made into a free town, and was used as a port by both Germany and Poland.

Czechoslovakia was created as a totally new state, as was Yugoslavia, although the official name of Yugoslavia was not adopted until 1929.

During the twenties and thirties there was a general move towards authoritarian governments in central and Eastern Europe. By 1938 there was only one state which could be called democratic – Czechoslovakia.

The most important threat to democracy came from the rise of fascism in Italy and Germany. Hitler, Germany's leader after 1933, rejected the changes in frontiers brought about by the Versailles Treaty of 1919. In particular, he wanted to regain those parts of west Prussia lost to Poland (the Danzig corridor) and to take over those areas of Czechoslovakia which had a high proportion of German speakers (the Sudetenland).

In 1938 Hitler threatened the Czech government over the position of the German minorities, indicating that he intended to take the Sudetenland areas by force. In the crisis which followed, the Prime Ministers of France and Britain met Hitler at Munich in September 1938, and agreed to allow his takeover of the Sudetenland territories. He, in turn, promised that this would be his final demand.

But in March 1939 the German army took over the rest of Bohemia and Moravia. Britain and France did not intervene.

The Second World War

In March 1939, Hitler turned his attention to Poland. He took over the free town of Danzig and demanded that the Danzig corridor should again become part of the German Empire. Poland rejected his demands. In September 1939, after making an alliance with Russia, Germany attacked Poland. Britain honoured her defence treaty with Poland and declared war on Germany.

Most of Eastern Europe was occupied by the German army during the war. However, Hungary, Romania, Slovakia and Bulgaria were allies of the Germans and Italians. In 1941 Hitler broke the alliance with Russia and invaded Soviet lands. After bitter fighting German troops were pushed back by the Red Army.

In May 1945 Germany finally surrendered to the combined armies of the Soviet Union, Britain and America. Central and Eastern Europe had been totally devastated by the horrors of war.

▲ On the 28th June 1919 the peace treaty with Germany was signed in the Hall of Mirrors at the Palace of Versailles near Paris. The Treaty of Versailles formally ended the First World War and set the new frontiers for Europe.

▼ The Versailles Treaty of 1919 was the first of the peace treaties to be signed ending the First World War. The treaties established the independence of Poland, Czechoslovakia, Hungary and Yugoslavia. Austria then declined as a major European power.

Eastern Europe after the Versailles Treaty (1919)

Newly Created States
- Poland
- Free town of Danzig
- Czechoslovakia
- Yugoslavia

National frontiers after 1919

LITHUANIA, Baltic Sea, EAST PRUSSIA, Danzig Corridor, GERMANY, POLAND, CZECHOSLOVAKIA, AUSTRIA, HUNGARY, TRANSYLVANIA, MOLDAVIA, ROMANIA, Black Sea, YUGOSLAVIA, Adriatic Sea, BULGARIA, TURKEY, ALBANIA, GREECE

▶ In the early part of 1941 German troops attacked Yugoslavia. German troops were welcomed in Belgrade, the capital, by a small number of Germans living in Yugoslavia.

Czechoslovakia 1919–1939

SUDETEN-LAND
POLAND
Prague
BOHEMIA
MORAVIA
GERM-ANY
SLOVAKIA
Bratislava
AUSTRIA
HUNGARY
ROMANIA

▨ Areas with a large German population
▬ Border of Czechoslovakia 1919–1938
▬ Border of Czechoslovakia after October 1938
▨ Area occupied by the Germans after March 1939

▲ Hitler enters Karlsbad in Czechoslovakia in October 1938. His troops took over the Sudetenland areas of Czechoslovakia in the same month. These areas had a largely German-speaking population who welcomed the expansion of the German Reich.

◀ After 1919 the frontier areas of western Czechoslovakia all had large German-speaking populations. The German Chancellor, Adolf Hitler, used this as an excuse for threatening the independence of Czechoslovakia.

▲ Josip Broz, later Marshal Tito, (right) is today President Tito of Yugoslavia. He was leader of the guerilla fighters in Yugoslavia after the occupation by German troops in 1941.

◀ Yugoslav partisans fought a bitter war against German troops after the occupation in 1941. In April 1943, this group of partisans was captured and shot.

The birth of Eastern Europe

Socialism prevails

In 1945 the Allies signed the Potsdam agreement which would decide the the future of central and Eastern Europe. Now that the Soviet Red Army occupied most of Eastern Europe, the communists soon gained political power.

Ministers of non-communist parties were forced out of office by 1949, and political systems based on the Soviet model were established. The Communist Party then became the only party with major political influence. Where there had been monarchies, for example in Romania and Bulgaria, the kings were forced to abdicate and go into exile.

Political unrest

As a result of so many political and economic changes in Eastern Europe, there has been a certain amount of political unrest. Although the working classes were now in a much stronger position under socialist rule, they objected when too many sacrifices were demanded of them.

In the GDR in 1953 building workers went on strike when they were asked to work harder for the same wages. This strike then developed into a general political revolt against the communist system and had to be put down with the help of Soviet troops.

An even more serious uprising took place in Hungary in 1956 and many people were killed. As a result, many Hungarians fled to western Europe. In the GDR many people left during the late 1950s to live in prosperous West Germany, and in 1961 the frontiers with West Germany and West Berlin had to be sealed in order to stop this serious drain of skilled workers.

In 1968 an attempt to introduce a more liberal type of communism in Czechoslovakia was stopped when the armies of five countries (the Soviet Union, Poland, Bulgaria, Hungary and the GDR) invaded. The leader of the liberalizing movement, Alexander Dubcek, was eventually dismissed from his post as First Secretary of the Communist Party.

Despite these setbacks, the communist system is now firmly established in Eastern Europe. All eight countries, except Yugoslavia and Albania, are members of a military alliance known as the Warsaw Pact, which was set up in 1955 to oppose the Western Alliance (NATO).

The same six countries set up in 1949 the Council for Mutual Economic Aid for economic planning and development. Yugoslavia broke off relations with the Soviet Union in 1948, and although still a communist state, pursues an independent policy. Albania also left the Soviet bloc in 1961 and established close political and economic ties with China, although these ties have now been broken.

Eastern Europe after 1945

Acquired by the USSR after 1945 from Germany, Czechoslovakia, Poland and Rumania

Acquired by Poland from Germany after 1945

Acquired by Yugoslavia from Italy after 1945

National frontiers after 1945

▲ After 1945 Soviet influence crept westwards. All the states of Eastern Europe had communist-dominated governments by 1948. Except for Yugoslavia, all the countries came under direct Soviet influence. Germany was split into two states after 1949.

▲ In February 1945 the three main Allied leaders – Churchill, Roosevelt and Stalin – met at Yalta to decide what should happen after the defeat of Germany in Europe.

▶ In 1955 the two Russian leaders, Kruschev and Bulganin, visited Yugoslavia to try and improve relations between the two countries. These had been bad since Marshal Tito (left) had broken with the Soviet Union in 1948.

◄ In October 1956 the Hungarians rebelled against Soviet rule, but the revolt was crushed by Soviet tanks. Hungarians in Budapest destroyed the statue of Stalin, a symbol of Soviet domination.

▲ In March 1968 Alexander Dubcek became First Secretary of the Czechoslovak Communist Party. He believed that there should be much more freedom in the communist system. In 1969 he was replaced by Gustav Husak.

▼ On the 21st of August 1968 troops of five Warsaw pact countries invaded Czechoslovakia to stop the reform movement which had developed under their leader, Alexander Dubcek. There was no armed resistance.

New life in the arts

The artist and the system

The position of the artist in Eastern Europe is a difficult one. Artists are not allowed complete freedom of expression, but are encouraged to follow the communist theory of 'social realism'. This means that they must put forward a socialist viewpoint in their work.

For example, a style of painting has developed which is straightforward and realistic, showing scenes from everyday life, particularly people at work. The communist theory is that this will help to educate a mass audience to socialism. However, artists are not allowed to portray the problems arising from socialism or to question the socialist basis of society.

This situation inevitably leads to clashes between individual artists and their governments although there are signs that Poland, Hungary and Yugoslavia are becoming more liberal in their attitude. Despite these problems, many talented artists have emerged from Eastern Europe.

The cinema is one area in which several Eastern European countries have gained an international reputation. The first was Poland, when in 1954 the famous director, Andrzej Wajda made his first film *A Generation*. This was the first of three films about Poland during the Second World War.

Czechoslovakia's film industry developed later. Milos Forman began making successful films in the mid-sixties but this was brought to an abrupt end with the invasion of Czechoslovakia by Warsaw Pact troops in 1968.

Jiri Menzel was another director from this period. His film *Closely Observed Trains* made a big impact abroad.

Light entertainment

The theatre has also flourished in Eastern Europe, although it too has had its problems of censorship. As with all branches of the arts it is heavily subsidized by the State and most theatres are run by the State or the local authorities. The aim has been to attract a mass audience by offering a wide variety of light entertainment as well as more serious plays and opera. As a result many more people go to the theatre than in the West.

Puppet theatres are a very important aspect of the cultural scene, especially in Czechoslovakia and Poland where they are intended for adults as well as children.

Perhaps the most important playwright of Eastern Europe is Bertolt Brecht. He returned to East Germany from America after the Second World War and founded the world-famous Berliner Ensemble in East Berlin in 1949. Ironically Brecht's plays were for many years more popular in western Europe and America than in the East, apart from the GDR itself.

▲ *Ashes and Diamonds* was the last film in a trilogy by the famous Polish film director, Andrzej Wajda. The film featured as its star the famous Polish film actor, Zbigniew Cybulski.

▲ *News of the Morning*, a painting by the Albanian artist Niko Progri, shows women reading the day's news during their break from work. Artists in Albania are supported by the State. Grants are freely given to anyone wishing to take time off work to take up painting.

▶ A Yugoslav artist works on a new cartoon film. These films are very popular in central and Eastern Europe. Poland and Yugoslavia are especially famous for their cartoon films.

▲ Constantin Brancusi (1876-1957) was a famous Romanian sculptor whose works are important examples of abstract sculpture. This figure of a bird was shown in an exhibition at the Tate Gallery in London in 1978.

▲ There are many art galleries and museums in Eastern Europe. This Romanian gallery in Bucharest contains many examples of modern art.

▲ Black Theatre is a form of theatre made famous in Czechoslovakia. The actors perform against a black screen wearing fluorescent clothes. The objects on the stage are also painted in fluorescent paint, so that they show up sharply against the black background.

► Leos Janacek (1854-1928) was a famous Czech composer, and one of the founders of a Czech national tradition in music. This is a scene from his first opera *Jenufa* (1904).

Preserving the old customs

A rich tradition

The customs of Eastern Europe are many and varied, reflecting the wide range of races and traditions, and traditional folk art and folklore are encouraged. Admittedly this is often done for the sake of tourists but there is also a feeling that it is necessary to keep alive the old traditions despite the social and political changes of the last thirty years.

Except in the very remote parts of Eastern Europe it is not usual to see people wearing folk dress in day-to-day life, but singers and dancers often wear national costume at celebrations, such as weddings. These costumes are usually hand-made and require a great deal of skill and patience to make. Folk dancing is also a common sight during festivals and celebrations, and most of the countries have national folk-dancing troupes which make tours abroad.

Associated with these folk traditions is a whole range of crafts which are still practised today. Hand weaving is particularly popular in the southern countries, where wool is plentiful. Woodcarving and basketwork are other popular crafts.

The Village Museum in Bucharest, Romania, shows the whole range of Romanian folk art in its original setting. In this open-air museum old village houses, built in the styles of the various regions of Romania, house many examples of her folk tradition.

New customs

A very important new celebration throughout Eastern Europe is May Day, held on May 1st. It is a national public holiday when big parades of workers and the armed forces march through the major towns. In the past the emphasis was on the military aspects of the parades, with processions of tanks and rockets. Today the emphasis is more on civilian processions, and the whole day is treated more as a festival for the family.

Two other important events in the Eastern European calendar are the Day of Liberation and the celebration of the October Revolution in Russia on November 7th.

The first holiday takes place on different days in the various countries according to when that particular country was liberated from the Germans in the Second World War. It is not, however, celebrated in Yugoslavia and Albania where they have their own liberation days.

New Year's Day in most of the countries is a bigger holiday than Christmas. Most people have New Year's Eve as the occasion for the biggest parties of the year.

There are also in most countries festivals to celebrate the coming of spring, usually at the beginning of March. In the wine-growing countries there are wine festivals, usually in September, to celebrate the beginning of the wine harvest.

▲ Did Dracula live here? The original Prince Dracula, Vlad III, was not a vampire, but was famous for impaling his prisoners on stakes. The formidable Bran Castle in the Transylvanian Alps is supposed to be where the original Dracula lived.

▲ Popular festivals often have a strong element of folk custom. This is the Festival of Masks in Bulgaria.

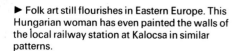

► Folk art still flourishes in Eastern Europe. This Hungarian woman has even painted the walls of the local railway station at Kalocsa in similar patterns.

◄ The Jews have had a great impact on the folk traditions of Poland. This is an example of Jewish wood carving.

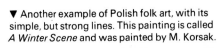

▲ Folk-dancing is an important part of the popular culture of Eastern and central Europe. As such it is encouraged by local and national organizations. This picture shows folk-dancers in southern Poland.

▼ Another example of Polish folk art, with its simple, but strong lines. This painting is called *A Winter Scene* and was painted by M. Korsak.

Religion and the State

Church and State

From 1945 to 1956, after the Communist Parties had gained power, many churches, especially the Roman Catholic Church, suffered persecution from the State. After 1956 this situation improved a great deal, and both institutions began to learn to exist side by side.

The Orthodox Church of Eastern Europe followed the example of the Russian Orthodox Church and supported the introduction of socialism in return for being allowed a certain amount of freedom.

The Roman Catholic Church, on the other hand, was much more critical of communist policies and has suffered more persecution because of this. Also the Roman Catholic Church is the only one ruled by a foreign head – the Pope in Rome. This has made communist leaders much more suspicious of the Catholics. However, although the Communist Parties continue to spread anti-religious feelings, generally the churches are tolerated.

The different religions

The two main religions of Eastern Europe are the Orthodox Church and the Catholic Church. There are over thirty million members of the Orthodox Church in Eastern Europe. The Roman Catholic Church is strongest in Poland, Hungary and Czechoslovakia.

The largest protestant Church in Eastern Europe is in the GDR, where there are fourteen million members. There are also four million Moslems in Eastern Europe, about half in Yugoslavia and the rest in Bulgaria and Albania. These mostly became Moslems at the time of the Turkish conquest in the fifteenth century.

Before the Second World War there was a huge number of Jews throughout the area, but millions were exterminated by the German Nazis, and a large number have since emigrated to Israel. Only Romania and Hungary have large communities left.

▲ The Orthodox Church is the national church of Romania. This Orthodox wedding is in a village in the Carpathian Mountains.

◄ The Jewish cemetery in Warsaw. Many Jews died during the German occupation and others emigrated to America or Britain. The Jewish population of Prague today is very small.

▼ The Roman Catholic Church is by far the largest church in Poland, but the Orthodox Church is also significant, especially in eastern Poland. This is the inside of an Orthodox church in Grabatka in eastern Poland.

▲ There are many old wooden churches and monasteries in the north of Romania, especially in Moldavia. This church dates from the eighteenth century.

◄ The Roman Catholic Church is very strong in Poland. This is an outdoor mass in a village near Cracow in southern Poland.

▼ This is the interior of a Moslem mosque in Pristina, southern Yugoslavia, where there is a large Albanian population, the majority of whom are Moslems. They were converted at the time of the Turkish occupation.

Equal opportunity for all

A new system

Before the Second World War, all the countries of Eastern Europe had different education systems, and education was usually restricted to middle and upper class children. The great political changes after the War meant that the system had to be completely reformed, a difficult task because of the different nationalities.

This was achieved by re-organizing the education systems along similar lines to the Soviet system. The aim was to make higher education open to everyone.

In general there is a greater emphasis on scientific subjects in Eastern Europe. In some countries, for example the GDR, there has also been a determined attempt to introduce schoolchildren to practical work in industry and agriculture. This was based on the Soviet idea and meant that in the GDR, for example, children from the age of eleven spent three or four hours a week working in a factory or on a collective farm.

This system has now been altered so that pupils no longer learn a specific skill during this period, but generally learn how the processes of production work. This means that pupils who go on to become office workers or teachers after their education still have direct experience of what it is like to work in a factory or on a farm.

Higher education is organized to meet the needs of the economy, so more importance is given to scientific and technical subjects, and the number of student places for arts subjects is restricted.

Higher education

Of course each country has its older, more traditional universities. The Charles University in Prague, for instance, was founded in 1348 and is therefore one of the oldest universities in Europe.

Since 1945, however, there has been a rapid growth in the number of technological institutes, where subjects are more closely related to the needs of industry and agriculture.

One of the main changes in higher education in Eastern Europe has been the large increase in the number of working-class students who reach university. This is a direct result of the policy of providing equal opportunity for all in the education system, and of giving each student an adequate grant to live on.

Another important aspect of the education system in Eastern Europe is the better provision of nursery schools compared to western Europe. The majority of children go to a kindergarten between the ages of three and six. In the GDR the figure is over eighty per cent. Many more women than in western Europe go out to work while their children are still young, so the provision of kindergartens and nurseries is very important.

▲ There are many nursery schools in Eastern Europe. Although these are not compulsory, most of the children attend. In the GDR the final year of the kindergarten is compulsory for all children as a preparation for the Basic 10-Year School. This kindergarten is in Prague, Czechoslovakia.

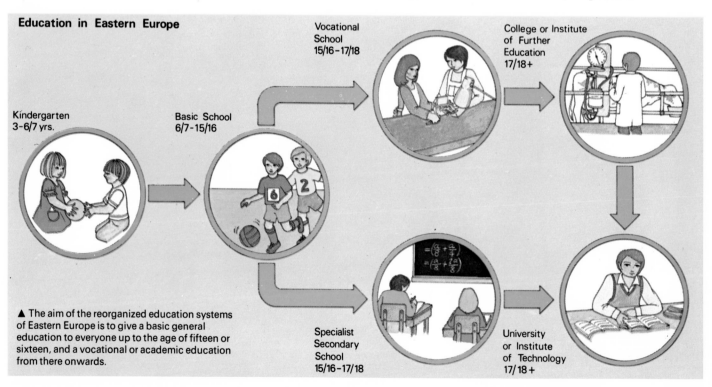

Education in Eastern Europe

Kindergarten 3-6/7 yrs.

Basic School 6/7-15/16

Vocational School 15/16-17/18

College or Institute of Further Education 17/18+

Specialist Secondary School 15/16-17/18

University or Institute of Technology 17/18+

▲ The aim of the reorganized education systems of Eastern Europe is to give a basic general education to everyone up to the age of fifteen or sixteen, and a vocational or academic education from there onwards.

◄ The physics room of the new apprentice school at Pelhrimov in southern Bohemia (Czechoslovakia). After leaving school apprentices spend part of their time working in a particular factory and the rest of the time at a similar vocational school, where they study both technical and general subjects.

▲ Medical students at the Charles University in Prague. There is a large proportion of female students in higher education in Eastern Europe, often studying subjects such as engineering.

▼ These are children at a Basic 8-Year School in Bucharest, Romania. Children often wear their Pioneer uniform to school, since many of the activities are organized at school.

The welfare states

Social welfare

Social welfare is one area where the states of Eastern Europe are far in advance of most other parts of the world. Most medical and social services are provided free, and in some countries workers do not even have to make contributions to the health and insurance funds since these contributions are made by the employer. There are, of course, variations between the eight countries.

The countries of Eastern Europe are particularly anxious to help families with children, for two important reasons. Firstly, several of the countries have experienced low birthrates since 1945, notably the GDR and Hungary. Secondly, a far higher proportion of women go out to work than in western Europe, so the state wants to make it as easy as possible for women to have children and then return to work.

Medical care

All the Eastern European countries have a national health service similar to that in Britain, but there is much less private medicine. There are some private doctors in the GDR, but the extent of private medicine as a whole in Eastern Europe is very small indeed.

Medical care is in general good with a large number of new hospitals. Some countries, notably the GDR, have introduced the Soviet idea of polyclinics. Instead of a patient going first to a local doctor and then being referred to a specialist at a hospital, he goes to the polyclinic where there are general practitioners as well as specialists in various different branches of medicine. The GDR has built 500 of these polyclinics in all the major and smaller towns.

There are also good medical facilities at factories in Eastern Europe, and many workers each year are allowed to have a free health cure at a sanatorium, paid for by the factory.

Pensions for old people

The amount of retirement pension varies from country to country, but on average it is about fifty to seventy per cent of normal salaries. In some countries, such as Bulgaria, the worker does not contribute towards his pension at all. This is done by the employer.

In Bulgaria the age at which a worker retires depends on the type of work he has been doing. Workers in heavy jobs, such as mining, retire at fifty whereas other workers are not allowed to retire until fifty-five or sixty.

The pensions in the GDR are lower than in other countries, about a third of normal salaries. Even so they are still higher than in Britain, although much lower than in West Germany, where a pensioner receives on average sixty per cent of his former salary.

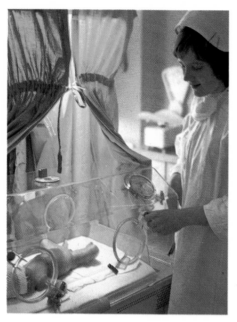

▲ All the countries of Eastern Europe have a national health service similar to that in Britain and all health treatment is free. In the more advanced countries of Eastern Europe, such as the GDR and Czechoslovakia, it is usual for babies to be born in hospital.

▶ A home for retired actors and actresses in Hungary. Women can retire at fifty-five and men at sixty. Their pensions are paid for by their employers and are usually about fifty per cent of their average earnings over the previous five years.

▲ A children's hospital in Czechoslovakia. Every care is taken to make sure that children are happy during a stay in hospital.

▲ Sanatoriums are often situated in mountain areas because of the clean, invigorating air. This sanatorium is at Szklarska Poreba in the Sudeten mountains in southern Poland.

▶ A sanatorium at Eforie Nord on the Black Sea coast of Romania. Workers are often sent to a sanatorium by their places of work for free treatment.

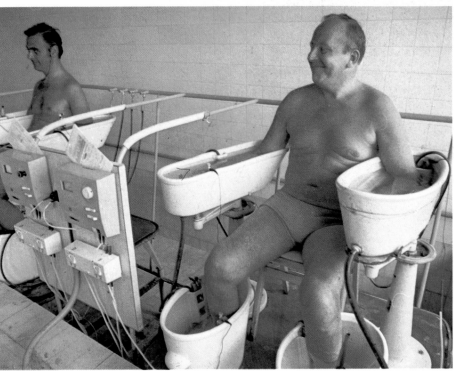

▲ Pensioners working in the garden of an old people's home in Czechoslovakia. It is considered important for old people to have some kind of work even though they are retired.

Rebuilding Eastern Europe's cities

The task of rebuilding

Poland and East Germany were the two Eastern European countries most affected by the ravages of war. Before the war, Warsaw had one of the most beautiful old towns in Europe, built mainly during the seventeenth and eighteenth centuries. After the war most of this area lay in ruins. The question was whether the old town could be rebuilt in its former style.

Fortunately there were in existence drawings and paintings of the whole of the old town by such artists as Canaletto which architects could use as a basis for reconstruction plans, especially for the facades.

The reconstruction work was started almost immediately after 1945, and by 1953 the old town market square had been completed. This was an enormous undertaking, especially during the most difficult post-war years. After more than thirty years, the work is now nearly finished.

Much of the rest of Warsaw consists of modern buildings which have been built since the war. In the centre of Warsaw the main new area is what is called the 'eastern side', the new town centre of Warsaw. Here a modern shopping centre has been built with large department stores. Around the centre have been built many new housing estates, such as the Za Zelazna Brama which is meant to house 15,000 people. To cope with the new traffic problems, two main through routes in the centre of Warsaw have been built.

At the end of the war, Berlin also lay in ruins. In 1949, two separate German states were created – the Federal Republic of Germany (West Germany) and the German Democratic Republic (East Germany). The eastern sector of Berlin became the capital of the GDR. Most of the central parts of the city had been badly damaged by bombing but it took longer for East Berlin to clear the rubble and start rebuilding.

With the help of money from America, West Berlin was rapidly transformed into a modern city, but East Berlin received no such help from the Soviet Union. It was only after the GDR had started to successfully develop its economy in the early 1960s that it could afford a large reconstruction plan.

The result is the redevelopment of most of the central part of East Berlin in modern style. The work is still going on, but the show-piece, the Alexanderplatz with its radio-tower and the Palace of the Republic, has now been completed.

There has also been a massive housing plan, with new estates in both the inner area and also in the suburbs. At the same time the older buildings of the city are being renovated, but this is a very slow process which will take many years to complete.

▲ Berlin in ruins at the end of the Second World War. Over fifty per cent of the houses were destroyed. This is a picture of the Brandenburg Gate which today is part of the frontier dividing East and West Berlin.

▼ The Alexanderplatz forms the new centre of East Berlin, which has been built over the last ten years. The main building is the recently completed Palace of the Republic, which houses cafes, theatres and restaurants. To the left of it is the new radio tower, which is 365 metres high.

▲ Renovation of old buildings is given high priority in East Berlin. The facades are given a face-lift and the flats themselves are provided with more modern facilities.

▶ This is the Central Station in Warsaw under construction. In the distance is the Palace of Culture which was built by the Soviet Union as a gift to the Polish nation after the Second World War. The architectural style is typical of the Stalin era in Eastern Europe.

▲ The Old Town of Warsaw was in ruins in 1945, but was restored almost exactly as it had been before the War. This is the market square in the centre of the Old Town.

▲ Warsaw is also a very modern city. The modern buildings here are the new shopping centre on Marszalkowska Street and Jerozolimskie Avenue.

▶ Canaletto's painting of Warsaw in the eighteenth century. The market square looks almost exactly the same today.

Industry

An industrial force today

In many ways Eastern Europe has seen far greater changes since the early 1950s than the more advanced countries of western Europe, whose industries developed in the nineteenth and early twentieth centuries. There are now modern industrial complexes throughout Eastern Europe which have drawn many of their industrial workers from jobs on the land.

More and more goods are now being exported. Poland, for example, is the eleventh largest shipbuilding country in the world, while Hungary is the sixth largest producer of bauxite, from which aluminium is made.

The GDR is world famous for its precision engineering, particularly the Zeiss factory in Jena which produces a wide range of precision instruments such as microscopes. Poland, Czechoslovakia and the GDR manufacture motor cars and buses on a large scale. Poland concluded an agreement with the Italian firm of Fiat in the mid-sixties to produce the Polski Fiat in Poland under licence. The GDR manufactures the Trabant and Wartburg cars, while Czechoslovakia exports many thousands of Skoda and Tatra cars each year.

Except for Romania, Eastern Europe is dependent on the Soviet Union for oil supplies. The 'Friendship' pipeline between the Soviet Union and most countries of Eastern Europe has been built to supply their oil needs.

The 'Adria' pipeline is also being built between Czechoslovakia, Hungary and Yugoslavia. Oil from the Middle East will be shipped to Yugoslav ports and then piped to the other countries except Romania. Romania is self-sufficient in oil and even pipes oil to the Soviet Union. Romania was the first commercial producer of oil in the world. The first oil well was dug at Ploiesti in 1857.

Eastern Europe is a major coal producing area, with Poland as one of the largest producers in the world and the GDR the largest producer of lignite (brown coal) in the world. Also important is the natural gas available in Hungary, Romania and Poland.

Industry and State

Almost all the important industry in Eastern Europe is owned and run by the State. Individual factories have had to work within a system in which most of the important decisions were taken by a central government authority, except in Yugoslavia.

Recently, however, there has been a move towards greater responsibility for individual factories, especially in Hungary. This has meant that workers' wages now depend much more on how successful their particular factory is and this has led to greater productivity and efficiency.

▲ Because of the increasing importance of technology in Eastern Europe, computers are being used in several branches of the economy. Computer firms from Britain and America are currently involved in helping the Eastern Europeans to develop their computer technology.

▶ An oil refinery at Ploesti in Romania. Ploesti is the centre of the Romanian oil industry, which is the largest in Europe after the Soviet Union. Romania is self-sufficient in oil and exports its surplus.

▲ Fiat cars being manufactured under licence in Poland. Several western car firms, such as Fiat and Renault, now have licensing agreements.

Eastern Europe's Mineral Wealth

— Oil pipelines
···· Finished products pipelines
○ Hard coal
● Lignite (brown coal)
● Oil
● Other major industrial areas

▼ Coal miners in southern Poland. Poland acquired the rich coalfields of Silesia from Germany after the Second World War and is now the third largest producer in the world after the Soviet Union and the USA. Poland's mines are equipped with the most modern machines available.

Excellence in sport

A love of competition

In the 1976 Olympic Games at Montreal the GDR won more medals than any other country in the world except the Soviet Union, which has more than thirteen times its population. The reason for its success lies mainly in the training, which starts from a very early age. Throughout Eastern Europe, sport is taken extremely seriously and is compulsory for children at school. Children who show great promise are transferred at an early age to specialist sports schools. One example is the swimmer Kornelia Ender, of the GDR. She was discovered at the age of eight, but retired from competitive swimming at the age of nineteen after winning four gold medals and one silver at the Montreal Olympics.

Sports stars also have a very high status in Eastern Europe. They can jump the queue for flats and cars and are also given leave from their jobs to concentrate on their training. At the end of their competitive careers they are often given good teaching jobs.

The success of the other Eastern European countries at the Olympics is not as outstanding as that of the GDR, but in general it is above average when compared with that of other countries in the world.

Football is by far the most popular playing and spectator sport in Eastern Europe. Eastern European countries which have been really successful at

football in the past are Hungary and Poland, who both qualified for the finals of the World Cup in Argentina. Czechoslovakia also has a good international reputation, and the other countries, except for Albania, have all achieved international honours both with national and club sides.

Gymnastics is one area of sport where the Eastern Europeans are especially strong. Czechoslovakia and Romania, with the incredible Nadia Comaneci, have been consistently successful at the Olympics, although they have had to compete with strong opposition from the Soviet Union.

Winter sports are also very popular, since all the countries of Eastern Europe have mountains where skiing is possible in winter. There are many skiing resorts in the Giant Mountains, the Tatras and the mountain ranges of Romania, Bulgaria, Yugoslavia and the GDR, some of which are used for international competitions.

Sport in general is very much encouraged by the governments of Eastern Europe. They put more money into the provision of sporting facilities than some Western countries, such as Britain. They feel that people will work better if they are healthier, as well as benefiting from the enjoyment of pursuing their favourite sports. Also, success in international sport is seen as an important element in gaining the respect of other countries in the world.

▲ Ice-hockey is a popular sport in Czechoslovakia and in Eastern Europe in general. International matches are eagerly awaited, especially between teams such as Czechoslovakia and the Soviet Union.

▼ The most popular sport in Eastern Europe is undoubtedly football. Both Poland and Hungary qualified for the finals of the 1978 World Cup in Argentina. This match is being played in Tirana, the capital of Albania.

▲ Kornelia Ender has broken twenty-three world records in swimming. At the Montreal Olympics in 1976 she won four gold medals and one silver medal for the GDR. She has now given up competitive swimming.

◄ Bulgaria is famous for its weightlifters. Several recent world champion weightlifters have been Bulgarians.

▼ Oberhof in the Ezgebirge Mountains in the GDR is one of the main centres for winter sports competitions in Eastern Europe.

Food from many cultures

Varied and exotic recipes

The wide variation in climate and racial mix in Eastern Europe means that there are great differences in the cooking of the individual countries.

In the south the Turkish occupation has left its mark on the cooking of Bulgaria, Yugoslavia, Albania and Romania. Here, the food tends to be highly spiced. Pork and beef are eaten but lamb is perhaps the favourite meat. It is very often made into different types of kebab, such as *shashlik*, pieces of lamb grilled on skewers with onion and green peppers.

In the north the food tends to be heavier with a high consumption of potatoes and dumplings and with pork and beef as favourite meats. The influences on cooking in the northern countries have been mainly German and Austrian. Pork dishes are particularly popular in the GDR.

Czechoslovakia's cooking has been strongly influenced by Austria, as can be seen by the popularity of such dishes as *Wiener Schnitzel*. There are, however, some very distinctive Czechoslovak dishes, such as fruit dumplings and carp cooked with garlic, which is the traditional food for Christmas Eve dinner.

Hungary has one of the most distinctive cuisines in Europe. Paprika is used in a large number of dishes, such as the world-famous meat stew, goulash, and the excellent Danube or Balaton fish soups.

Polish cooking has been strongly influenced by that of Russia, especially in its soups, such as *chlodnik*, a cold beetroot soup.

Wine and beer

The southern part of Eastern Europe is one of the most important areas in Europe for the production of wine. Hungary is the most important producer of quality wines, with a tradition of wine-making which stretches back many centuries. The most famous wine is Tokaj, a heavy dessert wine. Wine is a major part of Hungary's export trade, but a large amount is also drunk at home.

Yugoslavia, Romania and Bulgaria all produce and export large quantities of wine. Yugoslavia is famous for its white Riesling wines, such as the Lutomer Riesling from the north.

All four of the wine producing countries also make a very strong and fiery plum brandy. The most famous in the Yugoslav Slivovitz. By contrast, the northern countries of Eastern Europe produce and consume more beer than wine.

Czechoslovakia is the sixth largest producer of beer in the world, and the town of Plzen has given its name to a famous beer – Pilsner. The Germans are also famous beer manufacturers, and the GDR produces and consumes only slightly less beer than the Czechoslovaks.

▲ Vodka (literally 'little water' in Russian) is produced in Poland, as well as in Russia, from potatoes or corn. Most exported vodka is white, but vodka can be many different colours depending on the basic ingredient. Brandies made from fruit are very popular, especially in the southern countries of Eastern Europe.

▶ A Romanian woman cooking pastries in oil. They taste very similar to doughnuts.

Some Eastern European foods

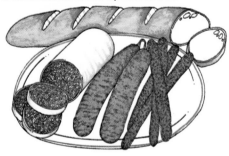

▲ Highly spiced sausage is an extremely popular food in all the countries of Eastern Europe. Hungarian salami (left) is one of the most famous.

▲ *Shashlik* is a very popular kind of kebab from the Balkans. Meat, peppers, tomatoes and onions are grilled together on a skewer.

▲ *Goulash*, a meat stew spiced with paprika, has become popular all over the world. Originally, it came from Hungary.

▲ A wine-cellar in Tokaj, Hungary. The cellarman is testing the wine from the barrels in which the wine is stored for several years. Tokaj is the most famous wine of Hungary.

▶ Wine labels from Hungary, Yugoslavia, Bulgaria and Romania are not usually as detailed as those from France, Germany and Italy, since most of the wine is produced by large state-run wine cellars, rather than by individual vineyards.

◀ A workers' pub in Hungary. Although Hungary is a major wine-producer, the average Hungarian also likes to drink beer.

49

Holidays and leisure

More leisure time

The majority of Eastern Europeans have three to four weeks paid holiday a year and most people spend at least some of that time away from home on a long vacation.

In the more advanced countries of Eastern Europe, especially in the GDR, Czechoslovakia and Hungary, there has been rapid growth in private holiday houses. These are very often only small wooden cabins with a minimum of facilities. They are usually built by the owners themselves, but they are big enough for a family to spend weekends and the summer holidays in.

Another popular kind of holiday is camping, with a car and tent. This is because hotel accommodation is limited unless you go in an officially organized group.

Places to go on holiday

It is difficult for the majority of Eastern Europeans to travel outside the communist countries of the Eastern bloc. Their governments do not encourage travel to western countries.

However, it is possible for citizens of some of the countries to take a holiday in western Europe and quite a few Czechoslovaks, Poles and Hungarians do. But their governments restrict the amount of foreign currency they can buy, so that unless they are able to stay with relatives or

friends in the West, they would find a holiday there very expensive.

As a result Eastern Europeans are restricted to a small number of countries for holidays although there are many areas offering different types of holiday activity to choose from.

If they prefer a seaside holiday they can go to the Baltic Coast in the north or to the Black Sea in the south-east. It may also be possible to go to the Yugoslav coast but since this has become popular with western tourists, prices tend to be higher.

In the last few years, the Black Sea coast in Romania and Bulgaria has also become popular with western package tourists, and some huge new resorts, such as Mamaia in Romania, have been built to accommodate the influx of tourists.

There are a large number of mountain areas in Eastern Europe such as the Giant Mountains and the Tatras in Czechoslovakia, which are popular for walking in summer, and for skiing in winter. There are also large skiing centres in the Transylvanian Alps and Carpathians in Romania, and in Yugoslavia and Bulgaria.

One of the favourite resorts of central Europe, especially for Hungarians, is Lake Balaton in north-west Hungary. It is the largest lake in central Europe. Since it is only 112 kilometres from Budapest, it tends to get very crowded in summer.

▲ May Day is a popular festival throughout Eastern Europe. Most people have a holiday on both May 1st and 2nd and take part in parades and celebrations.

▶ Hotel accommodation is quite scarce in summer, so camping is the most popular kind of holiday. These campers are in the GDR.

▲ A hunting party in Poland. Large areas of Eastern Europe are covered in wild forests, with wolves and bears in the more remote areas. Hunting of all types is a common leisure activity.

▲ A beach resort on the Black Sea in Bulgaria. The Black Sea is a favourite holiday area because of its fine beaches and warm, dependable summers. During the last few years many new hotels have been built to accommodate the influx of tourists.

▶ Chess is a popular game with all age-groups. There are many chess tournaments and clubs.

Reference: *Human and physical geography*

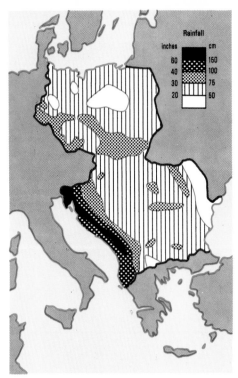

Rainfall and climate

The map shows how the rainfall in Eastern Europe is the heaviest along the Dalmation coast down into Albania and in the mountainous area of northern Yugoslavia, Czechoslovakia and Romania. The Adriatic coast, having a Mediterranean climate, has its highest rainfall in the winter, whereas the rest of Eastern Europe has most rain in summer.

The driest areas are in the GDR and Poland in the north and in the Hungarian Plain and the eastern part of Romania in the central regions. As far as the temperature is concerned, the coldest areas are the mountainous parts of Romania and Czechoslovakia. At lower levels, the coldest capital city is Warsaw. In summer the warmest parts are the coastal areas in the south, along the Black Sea and Adriatic coasts, and also along the Danube Plain. The further north and west you go, the cooler become the summers. The warmest capital city in summer is Tirana in Albania.

Population

Population is extremely unevenly distributed through Eastern Europe. Some areas have very little industry and the land is very poor, especially in the mountainous areas of central and northern Romania, central and southern Yugoslavia and Albania. In these areas the land can only support a small number of people and there are few other jobs. The population has therefore been forced to move elsewhere in order to find work.

The most densely populated area is the industrial strip which runs through the south of the GDR and southern Poland. Most of the western parts of Czechoslovakia are also heavily populated.

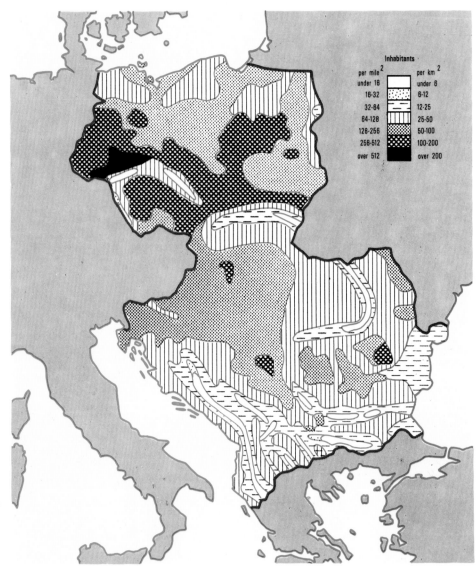

Populations of main cities

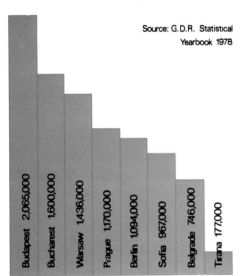

Source: G.D.R. Statistical
Yearbook 1978

Budapest 2,065,000
Bucharest 1,600,000
Warsaw 1,436,000
Prague 1,170,000
Berlin 1,094,000
Sofia 967,000
Belgrade 746,000
Tirana 177,000

▲ Budapest is the only city with a population higher than two million. There are no capital cities which can rival the size of Paris and London in Eastern Europe.

▼ The population of Eastern Europe is just over half that of the USSR and the USA, but it has a much smaller area. Its population density is therefore much greater. However, compared to the EEC, it has a lower population density.

Eastern Europe consists of a group of eight countries, sharing common interests and problems arising from their similar socialist systems of government. Yugoslavia and Albania have achieved greater political independence, but because of their socialist systems of government they are still regarded as being part of the Eastern bloc.

There are also racial ties between the eight countries, since the overwhelming majority of people are Slavs. These political and racial ties help to overcome the great difference in geography and climate between the countries.

▼ It would make an interesting journey to travel from the Baltic Sea in the north, down through the mountains of central Europe to the sunny climate of the Adriatic and Black Seas in the south. There is hardly any other part of Europe which could provide such a fascinating variety of scenery, people and climate.

Eastern Europe and others – population and land area

Eastern Europe
Pop. 130,500,000
Area 1,276,000
sq. km.

E.E.C.
Pop. 257,835,000
Area 1,528,200
sq. km.

U.S.S.R
Pop. 252,064,000
Area 22,402,000
sq. km.

U.S.A.
Pop. 211,909,000
Area 9,363,100
sq. km.

Source: Eurostat 1977,
G.D.R. Statistical Yearbook 1977

The eight countries – a comparison

▼ Poland has the highest population, but also the largest area. Its density of population is therefore similar to that of Yugoslavia and Romania, the next highest population. The most densely populated country is the GDR.

BULGARIA
Pop. 8.7 mill.
Area 111,000 sq. km.
Capital Sofia

CZECHOSLOVAKIA
Pop. 14.9 mill.
Area 128,000 sq. km.
Capital Prague

G.D.R.
Pop. 16.7 mill.
Area 108,000 sq km.
Capital Berlin

HUNGARY
Pop. 10.5 mill.
Area 93,000 sq. km.
Capital Budapest

POLAND
Pop. 34.3 mill
Area 313,000 sq. km.
Capital Warsaw

ROMANIA
Pop. 21.4 mill.
Area 238,000 sq. km.
Capital Bucharest

YUGOSLAVIA
Pop. 21.5 mill.
Area 256,000 sq. km.
Capital Belgrade

ALBANIA
Pop. 2.5 mill.
Area 29,000 sq. km.
Capital Tirana

Reference: *Agriculture*

Despite the increase in industrial production, agriculture is still a very important part of the economy of Eastern Europe, especially in the south. Although agricultural production lags behind that of western Europe, it is hoped that with increased mechanization and more widespread use of fertilizers, production will increase. Where collective farms have been introduced (all the countries except Poland and Yugoslavia) problems which arose from collectivization, such as inefficient planning and a reluctant work force, have mostly been overcome.

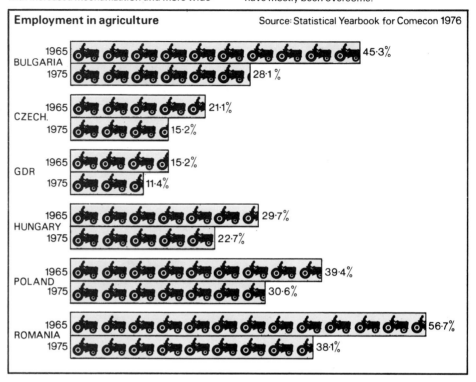

Employment in agriculture

Source: Statistical Yearbook for Comecon 1976

BULGARIA 1965 45·3%
1975 28·1%

CZECH. 1965 21·1%
1975 15·2%

GDR 1965 15·2%
1975 11·4%

HUNGARY 1965 29·7%
1975 22·7%

POLAND 1965 39·4%
1975 30·6%

ROMANIA 1965 56·7%
1975 38·1%

▼ Eastern Europe produces a wide variety of agricultural products, although the emphasis tends to be on the staple foods. Potato production, for example, is nearly twenty-five million metric tons more than in the EEC. Maize is also an important crop in Eastern Europe, more so than in the EEC countries. The EEC, however, produces far more wheat, barley, sugar beet and meat.

▲ The drop in the number of people employed in agriculture has been very steep, especially in Romania and Bulgaria. In the poorer agricultural areas, there were too many people working on the land, so many former agricultural workers have either moved into the towns or commute to the towns for work.

Agricultural production

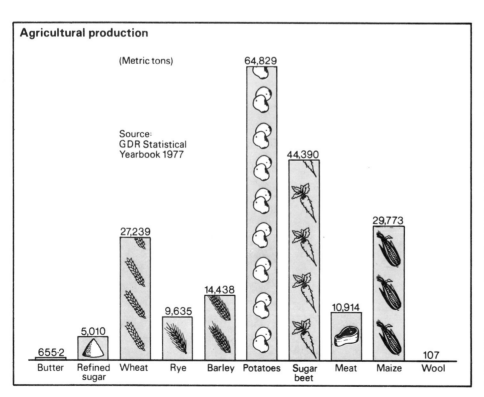

(Metric tons)

Source:
GDR Statistical
Yearbook 1977

| | 655·2 | 5,010 | 27,239 | 9,635 | 14,438 | 64,829 | 44,390 | 10,914 | 29,773 | 107 |
| Butter | Refined sugar | Wheat | Rye | Barley | Potatoes | Sugar beet | Meat | Maize | Wool |

Indices of agricultural production (excluding Albania)

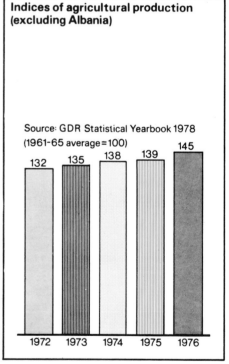

Source: GDR Statistical Yearbook 1978
(1961-65 average=100)

| 132 | 135 | 138 | 139 | 145 |
| 1972 | 1973 | 1974 | 1975 | 1976 |

▲ The growth in agricultural production has not been as high as had been hoped. Yields are still lower than in the west. However, there has been a strong improvement recently, as can be seen from the fairly sharp rise in output between 1975 and 1976.

Agriculture in Eastern Europe

Wheat		Principal Fishing Ports	
Maize and Millet		Cattle	
Rye		Pigs	
Rice		Sheep	
Potatoes		Flax	
Sugar Beet		Cotton	
Vinyards		Tobacco	
Orchards		Sunflower Seeds	
Olives			

Berlin

Warsaw

Prague

Budapest

Belgrade

Bucharest

Sofia

Tirane

Reference: *Industry*

Fifty years ago, most of Eastern Europe had very little industry. Only Poland, Germany and Czechoslovakia had important industrial enterprises. However, there had been rapid industrialization since 1945 and nationalization of all major industries. Eastern Europe now provides a significant part of European industrial production, and more attention is now paid to the quality of the goods produced. Eastern Europe is also now importing advanced systems of industrial technology from the West, such as computers.

Employment in industry

Source: Statistical Yearbook for Comecon 1976

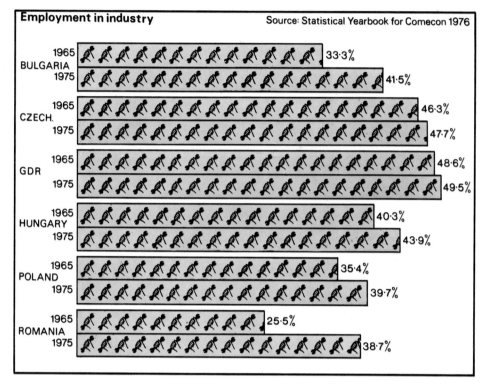

BULGARIA	1965	33·3%
	1975	41·5%
CZECH.	1965	46·3%
	1975	47·7%
GDR	1965	48·6%
	1975	49·5%
HUNGARY	1965	40·3%
	1975	43·9%
POLAND	1965	35·4%
	1975	39·7%
ROMANIA	1965	25·5%
	1975	38·7%

▼ The range of industrial production in Eastern Europe is now much wider than it was twenty years ago. Heavy industry is still most important although there has been an increase in light industry, especially over the last ten years. Production of pig iron and crude steel is less than half that of the EEC countries, but it does have one of the most important oil-producing areas in Europe, in Romania, and also one of the richest coalfields, in southern Poland.

▲ As the number employed in agriculture has gone down, so the number in industry has risen. Again the sharpest rises are in Bulgaria and Romania. Industrial processes in Eastern Europe, with the exception of the GDR, are not as automated as in western Europe, so the level of productivity tends to be lower.

Industrial production

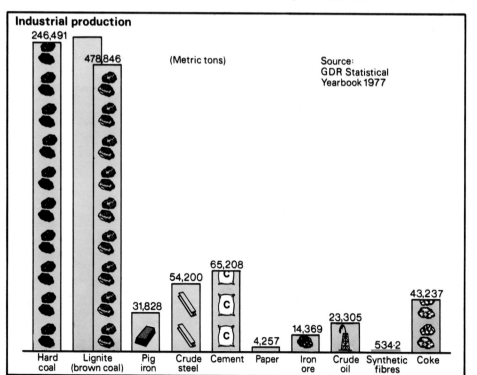

(Metric tons)

Source: GDR Statistical Yearbook 1977

Hard coal	Lignite (brown coal)	Pig iron	Crude steel	Cement	Paper	Iron ore	Crude oil	Synthetic fibres	Coke
246,491	478,846	31,828	54,200	65,208	4,257	14,369	23,305	534·2	43,237

Indices of industrial production (excluding Albania)

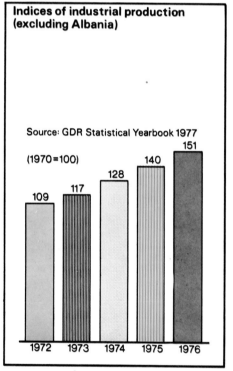

Source: GDR Statistical Yearbook 1977

(1970=100)

1972	1973	1974	1975	1976
109	117	128	140	151

▲ Because Eastern Europe was relatively backward industrially until the last twenty years, its development has been much more dramatic than western Europe's. Some of the problems of nationalization have been overcome and the rate of development in the 1970s has quickened.

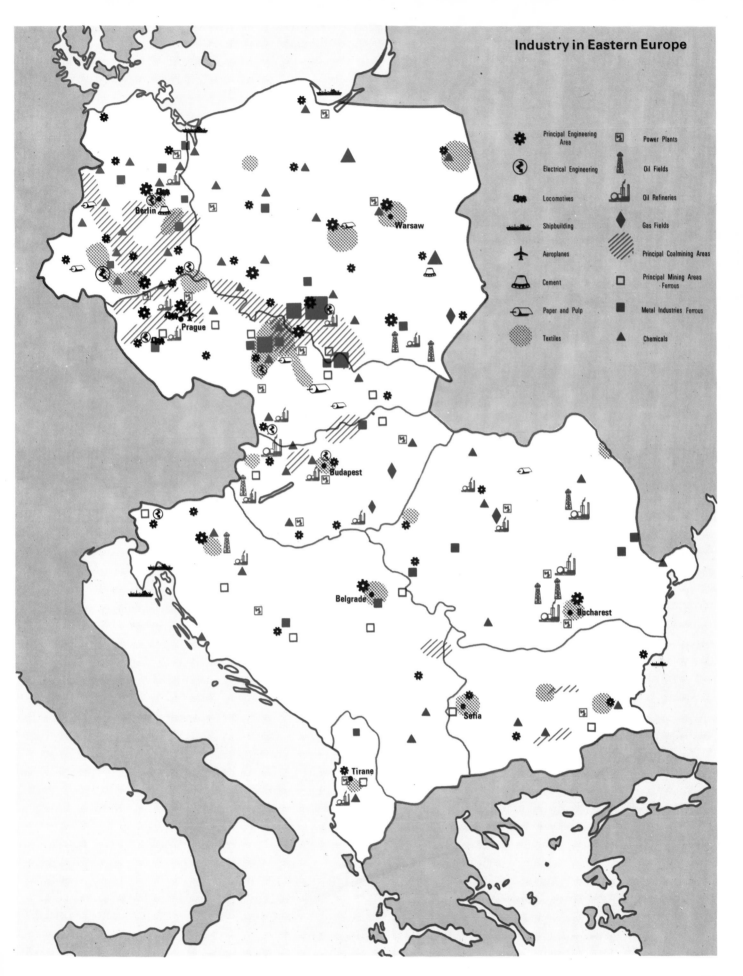

Industry in Eastern Europe

✿	Principal Engineering Area	▣	Power Plants
↻	Electrical Engineering	⬧	Oil Fields
🚂	Locomotives	⛓	Oil Refineries
⛴	Shipbuilding	◆	Gas Fields
✈	Aeroplanes	▨	Principal Coalmining Areas
⬯	Cement	▢	Principal Mining Areas Ferrous
⬭	Paper and Pulp	■	Metal Industries Ferrous
▒	Textiles	▲	Chemicals

Berlin

Warsaw

Prague

Budapest

Belgrade

Bucharest

Sofia

Tirane

Reference:
The economy

COMECON

The Council for Mutual Economic Aid (COMECON) was set up in 1949. It comprised all the countries of Eastern Europe except Yugoslavia, plus the Soviet Union and Outer Mongolia. In 1962 Albania left COMECON and in 1972 Cuba became a new member.

In the early years this organization had very little effect on economic planning between the different member states. However, after the political troubles of 1956, it was felt that long-term economic planning should be coordinated. It was decided that certain countries should concentrate on producing particular products or on particular sectors of industry and agriculture.

The creation of the Common Market in western Europe in 1957 made several of the countries think that COMECON should be made independent and self-governing, but this◙ idea was strongly opposed by Romania and was dropped in 1962.

The members of COMECON do the bulk of their trade with each other but recently there has been an increase in trade with other countries, especially with western Europe.

Economic organization

In the early years after the war the Eastern European countries followed the Soviet example and had highly centralized economic systems. Important decisions were made at a very high level, usually in a government ministry. Yugoslavia was the first country to break away from this system in the early fifties and give more independence to individual enterprises. The other countries followed this example later, in the mid- to late sixties, but they did not go nearly as far as Yugoslavia.

Recently there has been a move back to a more centralized system, although Yugoslavia has continued to assert her independence by not changing back. Yugoslavia also has more foreign trade with countries other than those in COMECON.

Agricultural production

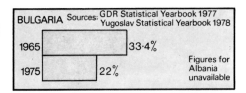

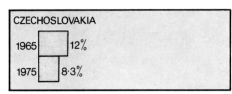

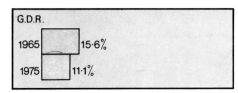

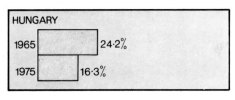

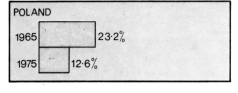

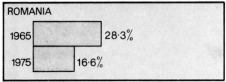

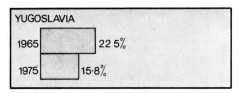

▲ Since 1945 the place of agriculture in the economies of all the countries has declined, although it still plays an important part. The relative decline has been greatest in Poland, Romania and Bulgaria. Bulgaria still receives the highest proportion of its income from agriculture compared to the other countries.

Industrial production has risen in all the countries except for Czechoslovakia. The rise in

Industrial production

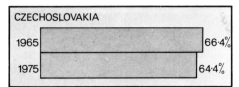

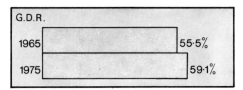

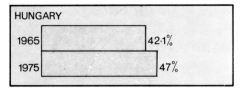

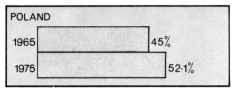

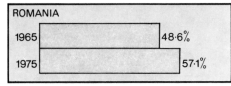

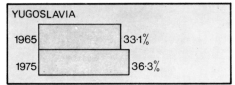

the proportion of national income from industry has been steepest in those countries which were basically agricultural before the Second World War, such as Bulgaria and Romania.

Yugoslavia's industry has not developed as strongly, and is still the most backward in this respect. Those areas of Germany which now form the GDR and Czechoslovakia already had an important industrial structure before the War.

► Foreign trade is important for all the Eastern European countries, since none is self-sufficient in raw materials. Since the convertible rouble (the rouble is the currency of the Soviet Union) was made the basic currency for trade between the COMECON countries in 1966, it has been easier for these countries to trade amongst themselves.

Trade with western countries is often hampered by a shortage of foreign currency in the COMECON countries, so the countries sometimes barter. A COMECON country may sell wheat, for example, in exchange for computers from a western country.

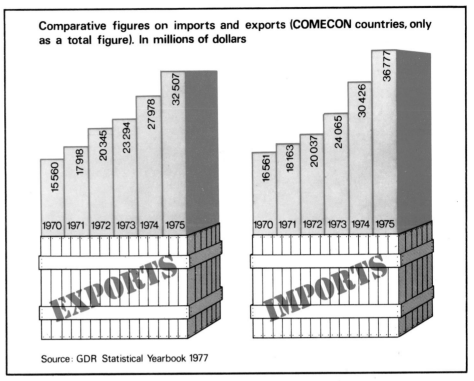

Comparative figures on imports and exports (COMECON countries, only as a total figure). In millions of dollars

EXPORTS

1970	1971	1972	1973	1974	1975
15 560	17 918	20 345	23 294	27 978	32 507

IMPORTS

1970	1971	1972	1973	1974	1975
16 561	18 163	20 037	24 065	30 426	36 777

Source: GDR Statistical Yearbook 1977

Production of various consumer goods, per 10,000 of population

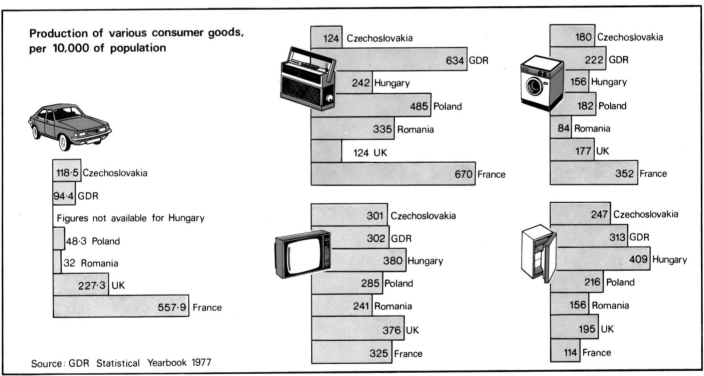

	Cars	Radios	Washing machines	TVs	Refrigerators
Czechoslovakia	118·5	124	180	301	247
GDR	94·4	634	222	302	313
Hungary	Figures not available	242	156	380	409
Poland	48·3	485	182	285	216
Romania	32	335	84	241	156
UK	227·3	124	177	376	195
France	557·9	670	352	325	114

Source: GDR Statistical Yearbook 1977

TV and radio licences per 1,000 of population 1975
Source: GDR Statistical Yearbook 1977
❋ Figures not available

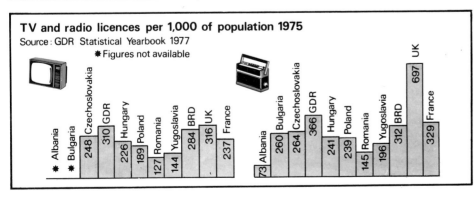

TV:
Albania	Bulgaria	Czechoslovakia	GDR	Hungary	Poland	Romania	Yugoslavia	BRD	UK	France
❋	❋	248	310	226	189	127	144	284	316	237

Radio:
Albania	Bulgaria	Czechoslovakia	GDR	Hungary	Poland	Romania	Yugoslavia	BRD	UK	France
73	260	264	366	241	239	145	196	312	697	329

▲ Although production of cars has risen recently, it is still below that of western countries. Production of the other consumer durables is, however, very much on the same level.

It will be interesting to see how the countries of Eastern Europe manage to cope with the increased demand for consumer goods, and whether they will be able to avoid some of the problems of the West, such as the traffic problems caused by almost universal car ownership.

◄ Ownership of basic consumer commodities is very similar to that of western Europe, with East Germany (GDR) leading the Eastern European countries.

The history of Eastern Europe

MAIN EVENTS IN THE HISTORY OF EASTERN EUROPE

A.D. 600 Settlement of Slav tribes as far west as the Elbe.

896 The Magyars occupy the Tisza and Danube Plain.

1453 The Turks capture the city of Constantinople.

1526 At the battle of Mohacs in Southern Hungary the Turks defeat the Hungarian army. Most of Hungary becomes part of the Ottoman Empire for the next 150 years.

1683 Vienna is besieged by the Turkish army. The Turks are, however, soon forced to retreat.

1699 The Turks are forced to leave Hungary.

1815 The Congress of Vienna. This establishes the frontiers of Europe for the next half-century.

1867 Austria and Hungary are split into two separate states, but retain a common foreign policy.

1871 Creation of a unified Germany under the leadership of Prussia and Bismarck, its prime minister.

1878 The Congress of Berlin ends the war between Russia and Turkey over the Balkans. It marks the beginning of the break-up of the Ottoman Empire.

1913 Albania becomes independent of Turkey.

1914 The assassination of the heir to the Austrian throne, Archduke Franz Ferdinand, in Sarajevo (June). In July Austria declares war on Serbia. This leads to the outbreak of the First World War.

1917 March and October Revolutions in Russia. The Bolsheviks, led by Lenin, seize power.

1918 Defeat of Germany and Austria-Hungary by Britain, France and Russia.

1919 The Treaty of Versailles is the first of several peace treaties between the victors and the defeated countries.

1919 War between Russia and Poland. Poland gains large parts of White Russia.

1933 Adolf Hitler becomes Chancellor of Germany after the National Socialists come to power.

1938 Hitler threatens to occupy those parts of Czechoslovakia with a strong German-speaking population. In September he meets the French and British Prime Ministers at Munich, and they agree to those areas being incorporated into the German Reich.

1939 March. The German army marches into the rest of Bohemia and Moravia. Slovakia becomes a separate state under German influence.

1939 September. Germany attacks Poland, after having made an alliance with Italy and a non-aggression pact with the Soviet Union. Britain and France declare war on Germany.

1941 Germany breaks its pact with the Soviet Union. Invasion of Yugoslavia by the German Army.

1944 Occupation of Romania, Bulgaria and Hungary by the Soviet army.

1945 February. Churchill, Stalin and Roosevelt meet at Yalta to decide on European frontiers and the administration of the defeated Germany.

1945 May. Surrender of the German Army.

1945 August. The four Allies – the Soviet Union, USA, Britain and France meet at Potsdam to finalize the administration of post-war Germany. Communist governments are set up in Yugoslavia and Albania.

1946 Coalition governments in Bulgaria, Poland, Romania, Hungary and Czechoslovakia are replaced by communist governments.

1948 Blockade by the Soviet Union of routes across East Germany to West Berlin. The blockade is overcome by an Anglo-American airlift.

1948 Yugoslavia, under Marshal Tito, breaks with the Soviet Union.

1949 Creation of the two German states; the GDR (East Germany) and the Federal Republic (West Germany).

1949 Foundation of the Council for Mutual Economic Aid (COMECON).

1950 Recognition by the GDR of the Oder-Neisse line as the frontier between Poland and the GDR.

1953 March. Josef Stalin dies. Strikes by workers in East Berlin lead to unrest throughout the GDR. Revolt put down by Soviet tanks.

1955 Creation of the Warsaw Pact, a military alliance between the Eastern European countries and the Soviet Union. Yugoslavia refuses to join.

1956 June. Riots in several Polish cities. As a result, Gomulka, a more liberal communist, gains power.

1956 October. A national uprising in Hungary is put down by the Soviet Army.

1961 The division of Germany is sealed by the building of Berlin Wall.

1962 Albania leaves COMECON.

1968 Invasion of Czechoslovakia by five countries of the Warsaw Pact. (The Soviet Union, the GDR, Poland, Bulgaria and Hungary.) Romania refuses to take part. Albania leaves the Warsaw pact in protest at the invasion of Czechoslovakia.

1971 A basic treaty is concluded between East and West Germany, in which the two German states formally recognize each other's existence.

1973 Both the GDR and the Federal Republic of Germany become members of the United Nations.

1973 The Helsinki agreement on European security between the states of Europe.

1977 The 'Charter 77' group in Czechoslovakia issues a charter on human rights based on the Helsinki agreement of 1973.

1978 A Pole, Cardinal Karol Wojtyla, becomes Pope.

Index

EAST EUROPE   Physical

International Boundaries

Cities and Towns

feet		metres
9000		2743
6000		1829
3000		914
1000		305
500		152
0		

Mountain Peaks
(in feet)

▲ 9560

below sea level

Scale 1:7,200,000

0   100 miles

0   100   200 kilometres

Projection: Conical Orthomorphic

M. & T.